BUTTERFLIES

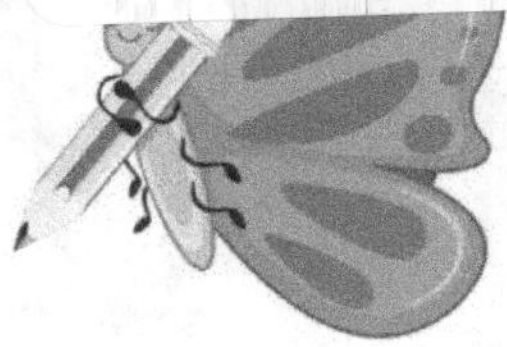

Coloring Book For Kids
Age 4 - 8

Soon, the warm sunny days of summer will be here. That will mean more time outside, playing in parks with friends, outdoor sports and maybe even wandering out into nature. If you're lucky, you might get to see a butterfly or two, either outdoors or at a botanical garden. Time to brush up on your butterfly knowledge.

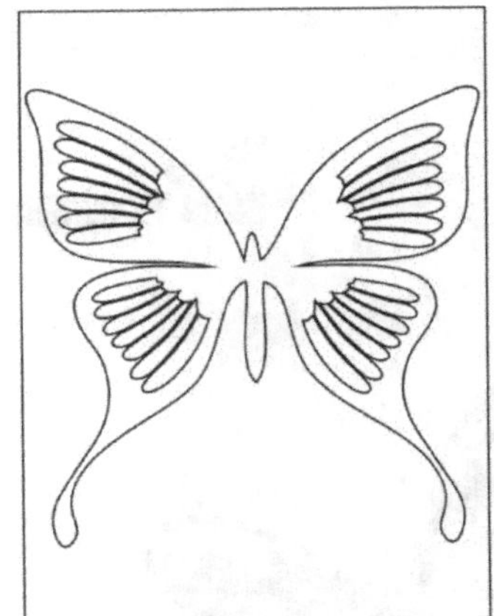

BUTTERFLIES
Coloring Book

This Book Belongs To:

Draw something

Female butterflies make a special sticky fluid that works like glue. They use it to attach their eggs to plants. The glue helps keep the eggs stuck in place. In fact, the eggs would be destroyed if anything tried to remove them from the plant. Once the eggs are attached to a leaf, a butterfly doesn't stay to care for its young. But it does carefully plan where it lays its eggs. It only chooses plants that will provide caterpillars with plenty to eat when they eventually hatch from their eggs.

Draw something

Long ago, Dutch scientists were studying butterflies. And they took a look at their poop — which is officially called frass. They noticed that the droppings looked an awful lot like butter. So they gave the insect the name butterfly. Some people suggest there's another explanation for the name of these beautiful bugs. At one time, it was believed that witches turned themselves into butterflies and then flew off in search of food, especially butter.

Draw something

It might sound strange to us humans, but butterflies rely on their feet to taste food. Their feet have taste sensors on them that help to locate food for their caterpillars. They stand on a leaf and give it a taste. If they determine the plant is something their caterpillars can eat, they'll lay their eggs in this spot. As for how butterflies themselves eat? They can't bite or chew. So butterflies use a long, tube-like tongue called a proboscis (say "pro-boss-kiss") to eat. It works like a straw, allowing butterflies to slurp up liquids like nectar, sap and juice from rotting fruit.

Draw something

Butterflies are an insect that lives anywhere from 2 days to as long as 11 months. They go through a four-step process called metamorphosis – from egg to caterpillar, to chrysalis to a butterfly.

Draw something

Most female butterflies lay their eggs on the kinds of plants their caterpillars will want to eat – this helps make sure the young are able to start eating right after they hatch. Otherwise, they will starve.

Draw something

Some butterfly eggs hatch in a few days; others in a few months. The average is 8 days.

Draw something

When a caterpillar reaches full size, it will molt to reveal a soft new body called a prepupa. The caterpillar spins silk and attaches itself to a twig or stick. His new soft body will harden to form a chrysalis.

Some butterflies hibernate during the winter – in caves, under leaves, inside houses, and other safe places.

Draw something

In North America, thousands of monarch butterflies migrate 1,800 miles each fall to spend the cold months on the coast of California or in Mexico. They travel about 80 miles per day!

Draw something

Butterflies flap all their wings at the same time at about 5 beats per second.

Draw something

A butterfly "tongue" is called a proboscis. Some sip flower nectar, tree sap, or salts and minerals from damp soil and puddles. Others may drink the liquid from decaying fruit (and even animal droppings!).

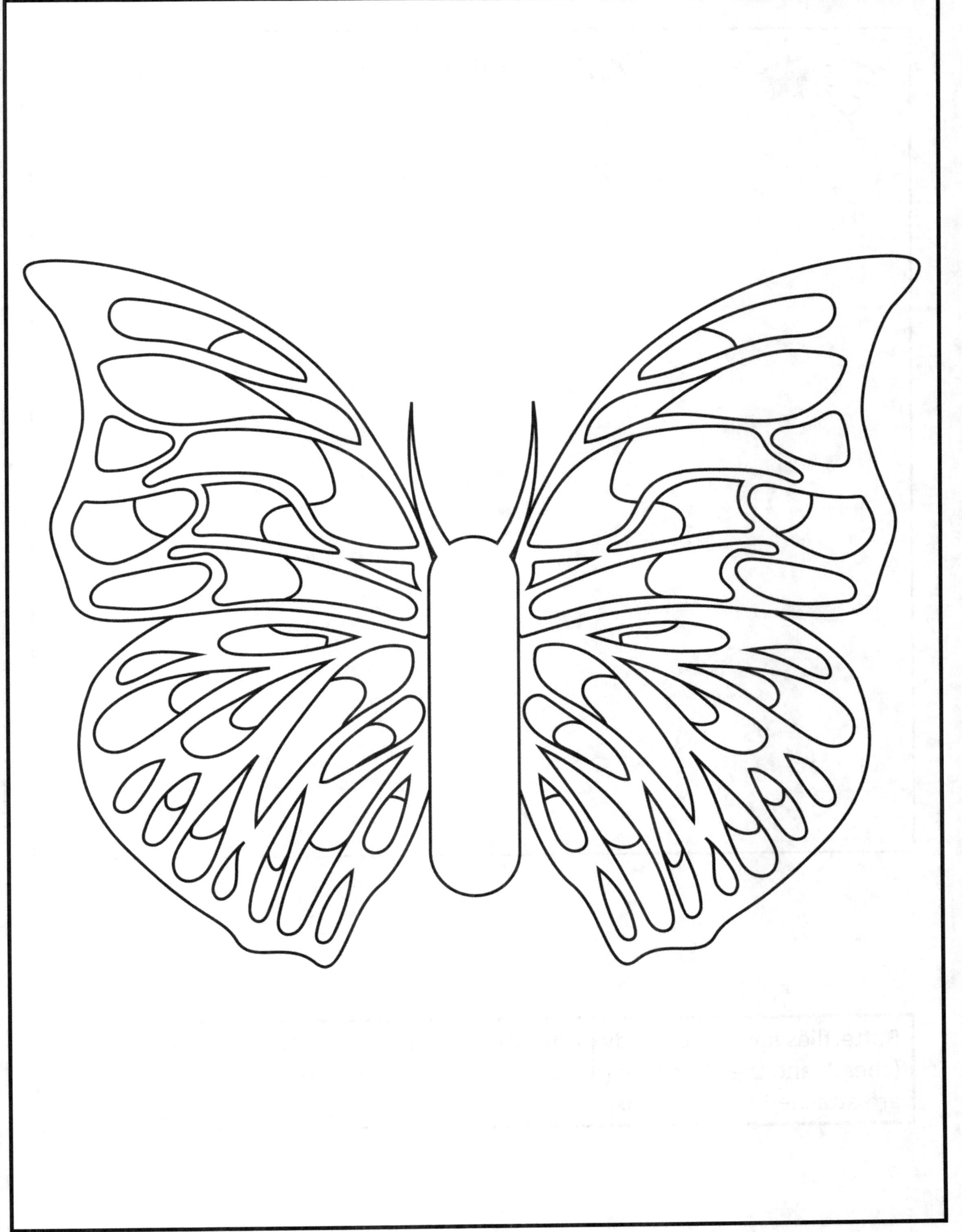

Draw something

Butterflies have three body parts, like all other insects: the head, the thorax (chest), and the abdomen (bottom). The butterfly's four wings and six legs are attached to the thorax.

Draw something

Scientists estimate that there are 28,000 species of butterflies throughout the world.

Draw something

Butterflies are colorful for many reasons. The colors help them attract a mate and absorb heat and the color also helps them blend in among the flowers when they are feeding.

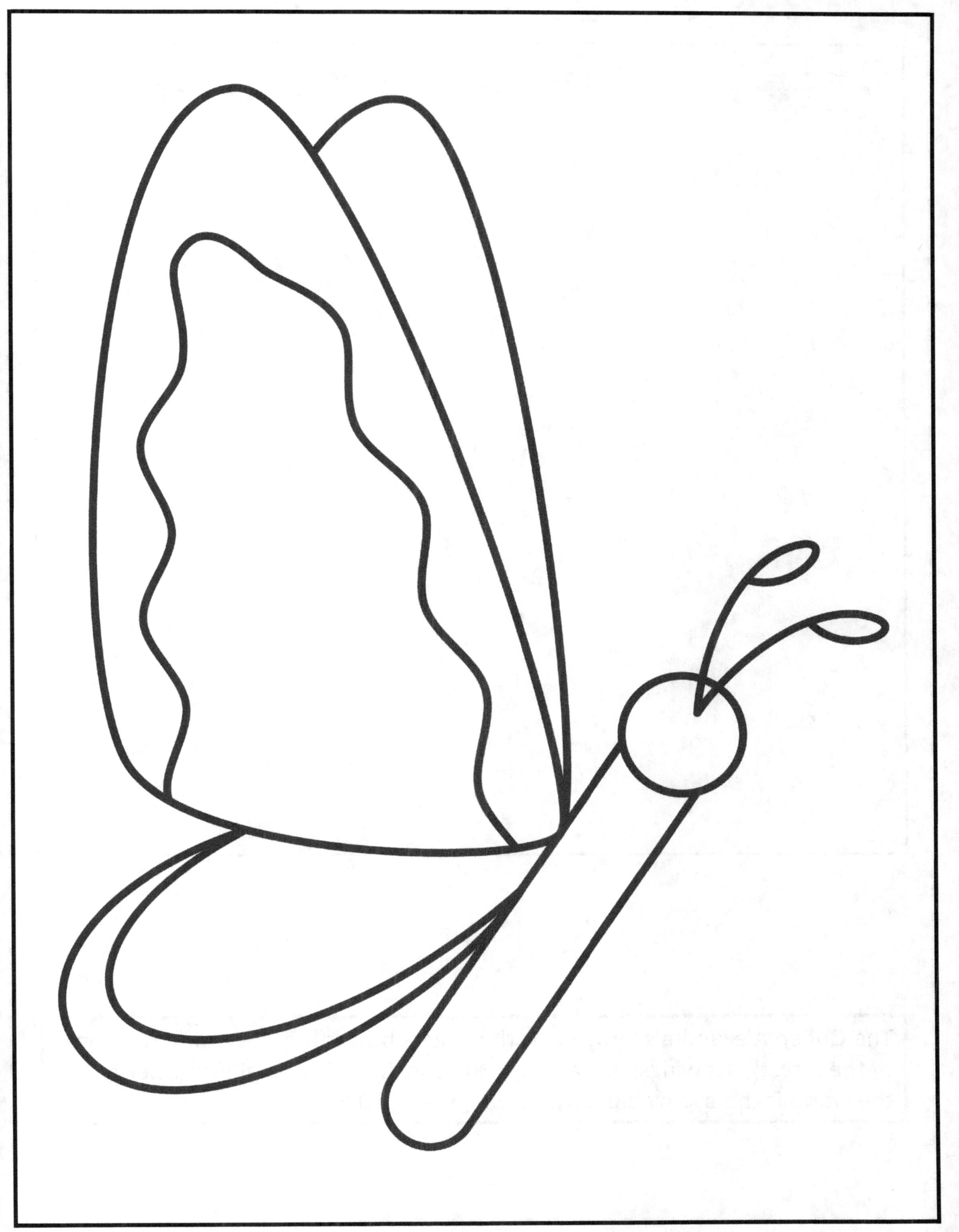

Draw something

The Queen Alexandra's Birdwing is the largest butterfly in the world (and one of the rarest). Its wingspan can grow to 11 inches! The smallest butterfly in the world is the pygmy blue, with a wingspan of 0.5 inches.

Draw something

Butterfly Wings Are Transparent
How can that be? We know butterflies as perhaps the most colorful, vibrant insects around! Well, a butterfly's wings are covered by thousands of tiny scales, and these scales reflect light in different colors. But underneath all of those scales, a butterfly wing is actually formed by layers of chitin—the same protein that makes up an insect's exoskeleton. These layers are so thin you can see right through them. As a butterfly ages, scales fall off the wings, leaving spots of transparency where the chitin layer is exposed.

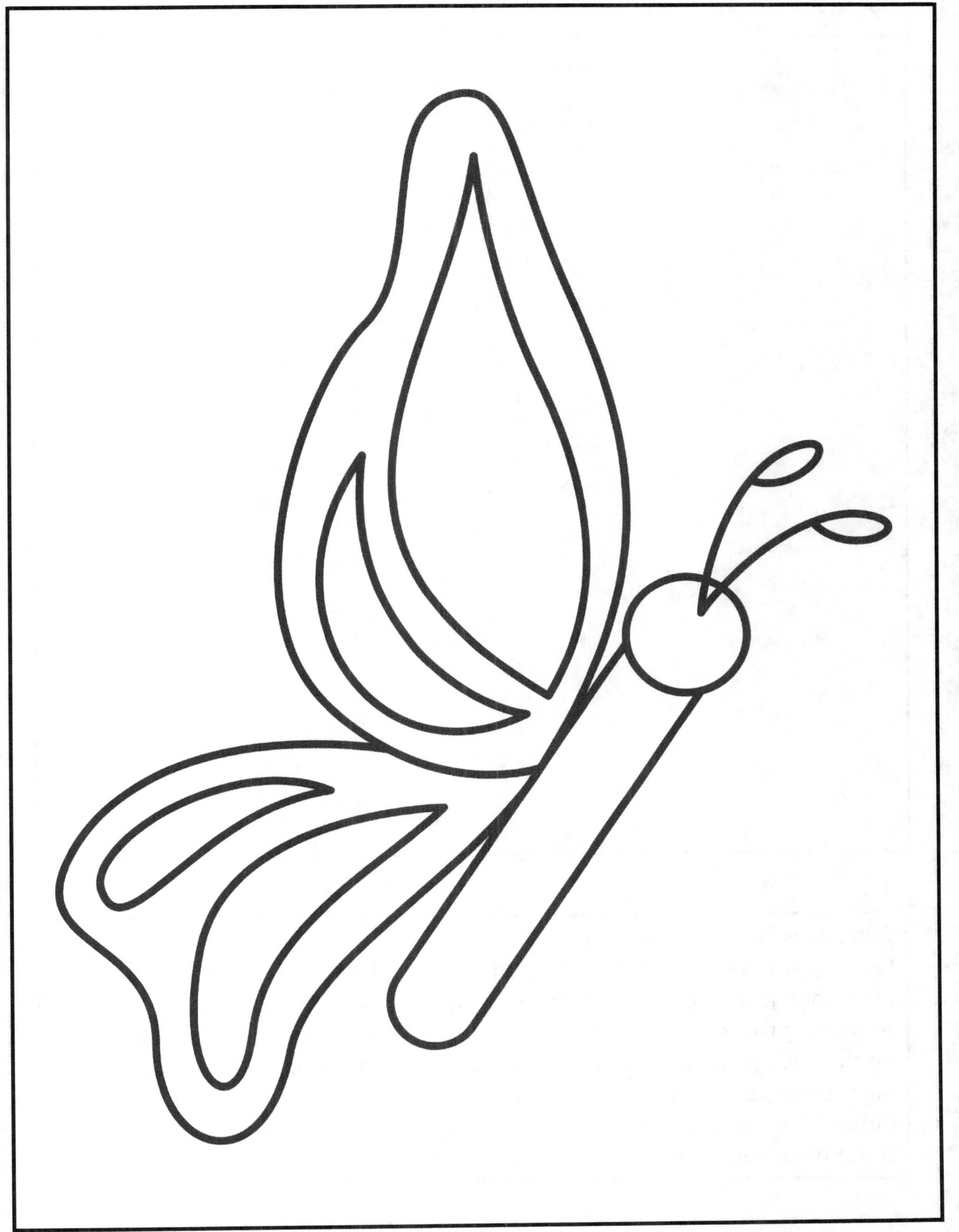

Draw something

Butterflies Taste With Their Feet
Butterflies have taste receptors on their feet to help them find their host plants and locate food. A female butterfly lands on different plants, drumming the leaves with her feet until the plant releases its juices. Spines on the back of her legs have chemoreceptors that detect the right match of plant chemicals. When she identifies the right plant, she lays her eggs. A butterfly of any biological sex will also step on its food, using organs that sense dissolved sugars to taste food sources like fermenting fruit.

Draw something

Butterflies Live on an All-Liquid Diet
Speaking of butterflies eating, adult butterflies can only feed on liquids—usually nectar. Their mouthparts are modified to enable them to drink, but they can't chew solids. A proboscis, which functions as a drinking straw, stays curled up under the butterfly's chin until it finds a source of nectar or other liquid nutrition. The long, tubular structure then unfurls and sips up a meal. A few species of butterflies feed on sap, and some even resort to sipping from carrion. No matter the meal, they suck it up a straw.

Draw something

Antarctica is the only continent on which no Lepidoptera have been found.

Draw something

Butterflies Drink From Mud Puddles
A butterfly cannot live on sugar alone; it needs minerals, too. To supplement its diet of nectar, a butterfly will occasionally sip from mud puddles, which are rich in minerals and salts. This behavior, called puddling, occurs more often in male butterflies, which incorporate the minerals into their sperm. These nutrients are then transferred to the female during mating and help improve the viability of her eggs.

Draw something

The most common butterfly in the US is the Cabbage White.
Named for its mostly white marking, when hints of yellow and green like the vegetable, the Cabbage White may not be the most colorful butterfly in your garden or yard, but it is the most common. The male Cabbage White has one prominent black spot on each wing, while the female has two.

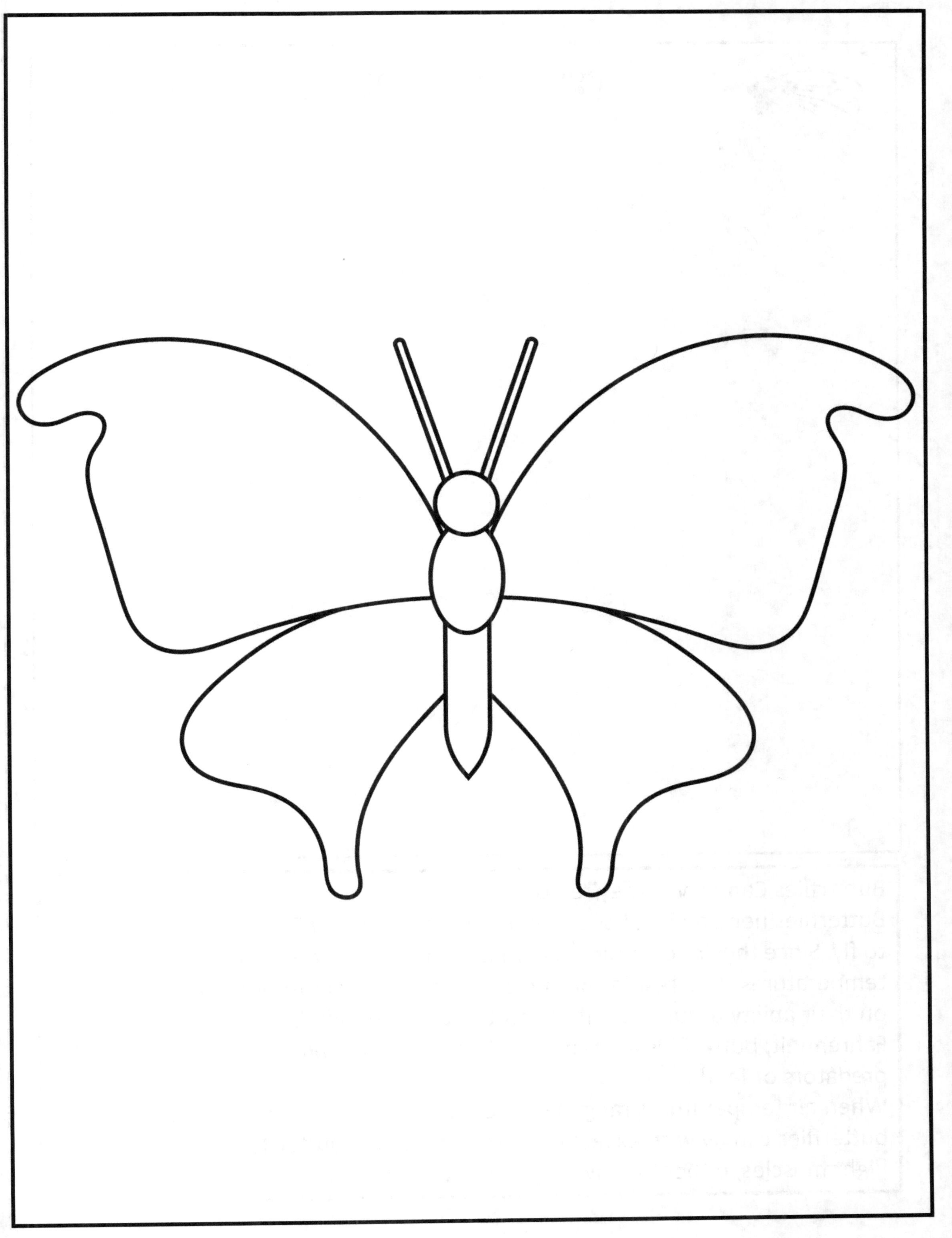

Draw something

Butterflies Can't Fly If They're Cold

Butterflies need an ideal body temperature of about 85 degrees Fahrenheit to fly. Since they're cold-blooded animals, they can't regulate their own body temperatures. As a result, the surrounding air temperature has a big impact on their ability to function. If the air temperature falls below 55 degrees Fahrenheit, butterflies are rendered immobile—unable to flee from predators or feed.

When air temperatures range between 82 and 100 degrees Fahrenheit, butterflies can fly with ease. Cooler days require a butterfly to warm up its flight muscles, either by shivering or basking in the sun.

Draw something

A Newly Emerged Butterfly Can't Fly

Inside the chrysalis, a developing butterfly waits to emerge with its wings collapsed around its body. When it finally breaks free of the pupal case, it greets the world with tiny, shriveled wings. The butterfly must immediately pump body fluid through its wing veins to expand them. Once its wings reach their full size, the butterfly must rest for a few hours to allow its body to dry and harden before it can take its first flight.

Draw something

Butterflies Employ Tricks to Avoid Being Eaten
Butterflies rank pretty low on the food chain, with lots of hungry predators happy to make a meal of them. Therefore, they need some defense mechanisms. Some butterflies fold their wings to blend into the background, using camouflage to render themselves all but invisible to predators. Others try the opposite strategy, wearing vibrant colors and patterns that boldly announce their presence. Bright colored insects often pack a toxic punch if eaten, so predators learn to avoid them.

Draw something

How do butterflies breathe? They don't have a nose or even lungs. Butterflies have tiny holes called spiracles on their outer skeleton (or exoskeleton), through which they breathe in oxygen.

They have compound eyes which gives them a wide field vision and allows them to see the Ultraviolet light which humans cannot see.

Draw something

Once a female butterfly lays its eggs on a plant, generally only one out of the hundreds survive.

Draw something

It takes a few weeks for the egg to hatch and the tiny caterpillar or larva crawls out of its egg. It begins by eating its eggshell and survives on eating leaves as most species are herbivores.

Draw something

One of the largest butterflies is the Giant Swallowtail Butterfly.
With a wingspread of between four and seven inches, this species has a name that fits its dimensions. If you have ever seen one on a hike or around your yard, you may have been spellbound by the sight of it. Their swallowtail description is borrowed from birds of the same name, thanks to the long tails on this butterfly's hindwings.

Draw something

The caterpillar eats and grows until it turns its biggest size and finally sheds its outer skin to reveal a hard-inner skin which is like a protective shell. At this time it attaches itself to a plant, generally the underside of a leaf. This is an exciting time because here's where it undergoes metamorphosis until it develops wings.

Draw something

After emerging out of the hard shell called chrysalis, this now adult butterfly has soft crumpled wings. It has to let them dry and has blood flow in them before it can fly, fly away!

Draw something

Behavior of Butterflies

Butterflies play a crucial role in flower pollination. Their feet help them to taste their food as well as smell to help in mating.

Most butterflies spend their lifetimes eating and mating.

The females lay eggs on the plants that would be a good meal for the future caterpillars.

A butterfly can see things up to 12 feet far, and anything farther becomes blurry. They mostly see reds, greens, and yellows.

They use the colors on their wings to camouflage in the plants and also to attract potential mates in their close radius.

Draw something

Butterflies are insects and are born as a crawling 'caterpillar'.

Draw something

Do They Migrate?
Some long-living species like the Monarch butterfly are known to migrate long distances like a thousand miles to shift base to a warmer region in winters.
They fly from Great Lakes all the way to the Gulf of Mexico.
A single butterfly can never make the entire journey, and it takes about 5-6 generations of the butterflies to migrate to their destination, from where they make a return during the spring.

Draw something

How Do They Protect Themselves?
Even though the majority of butterflies do not need to protect themselves for too long owing to their short lifespan, they have their clever defence mechanisms handy.
- The most common way of protection is hiding in plain sight. Yes, camouflage.
- Some butterflies like the Monarch can also make itself taste mad for its predator.
- Other witty ways of defense are bad smell and mimicry of the toxic variety.
The scales on their wings are easy to come off, and it makes it easy for them to slip out of a predator's grip.
- The flying pattern and speed also help them to get off the birds' radar.

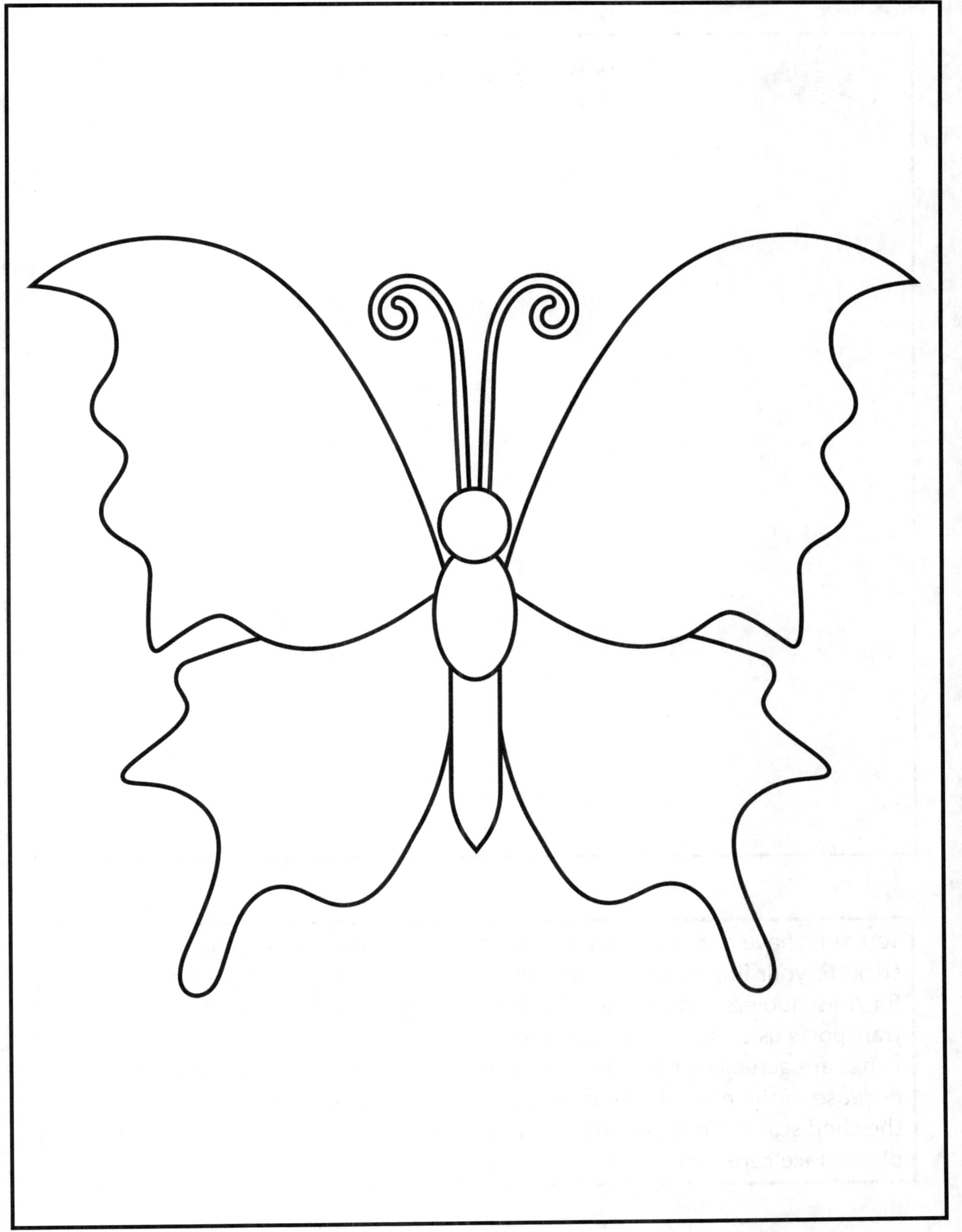

Draw something

You must have noticed that the color of a butterfly's wings comes off and sticks to your fingers when you hold it. One of the interesting butterfly facts for preschoolers is the reason for this. The sight of their colorful wings transports us to our childhoods no matter what age we are. A butterfly's wings are actually a translucent membrane. The colors that we see are because of the many scales on them. That color on our fingers is nothing but the shed scales. They can still fly, but if you're just trying to show some love, please take care that you touch and hold it gently.

Draw something

The antenna has light receptors which help them determine whether it's day or night. These also aid them in navigation and guidance with their direction of flying.

Draw something

In ancient Egyptian frescoes, butterfly representations are found that date about 3500 years back. It is said that they have been around for over

Draw something

The Monarch butterfly eats milkweed so that it tastes bad to one who tries to eat it.

Draw something

One of the earliest signs of spring is spotting a brimstone butterfly which can survive the winter.

Draw something

The female butterflies are generally bigger in size than the males, and they also live longer.

Draw something

Unfortunately, some species of butterflies are endangered, and some have already become extinct.

Draw something

There are seven families of butterflies under the Rhopalocera suborder. They are Hedylidae, Hesperiidae, Lycaenidae, Nymphalidae, Papilionidae, Pieridae and Riodinidae.

Draw something

The Blue Morpho butterfly is very expensive, it's sought after by wealthy individuals who collect butterflies

If you've ever touched a butterfly's wings, you may have gotten some dust on your fingers. This isn't dust, but scales that shed from a butterfly's wings over its lifespan. While this won't kill a butterfly, it's recommended you avoid touching its wings.

Draw something

You can buy butterfly habitats online and raise butterflies in your home or classroom.

Draw something

Lepidopterology is the study of butterflies and someone who studies lepidopterology is called a lepidopterist.

Draw something

The Morgan's Sphinx Moth from Madagascar has a proboscis (tube mouth) that is 12 to 14 inches long to get the nectar from the bottom of a 12-inch deep orchid discovered by Charles Darwin.

Draw something

Scientists estimate that there are 28,000 species of butterflies throughout the world.

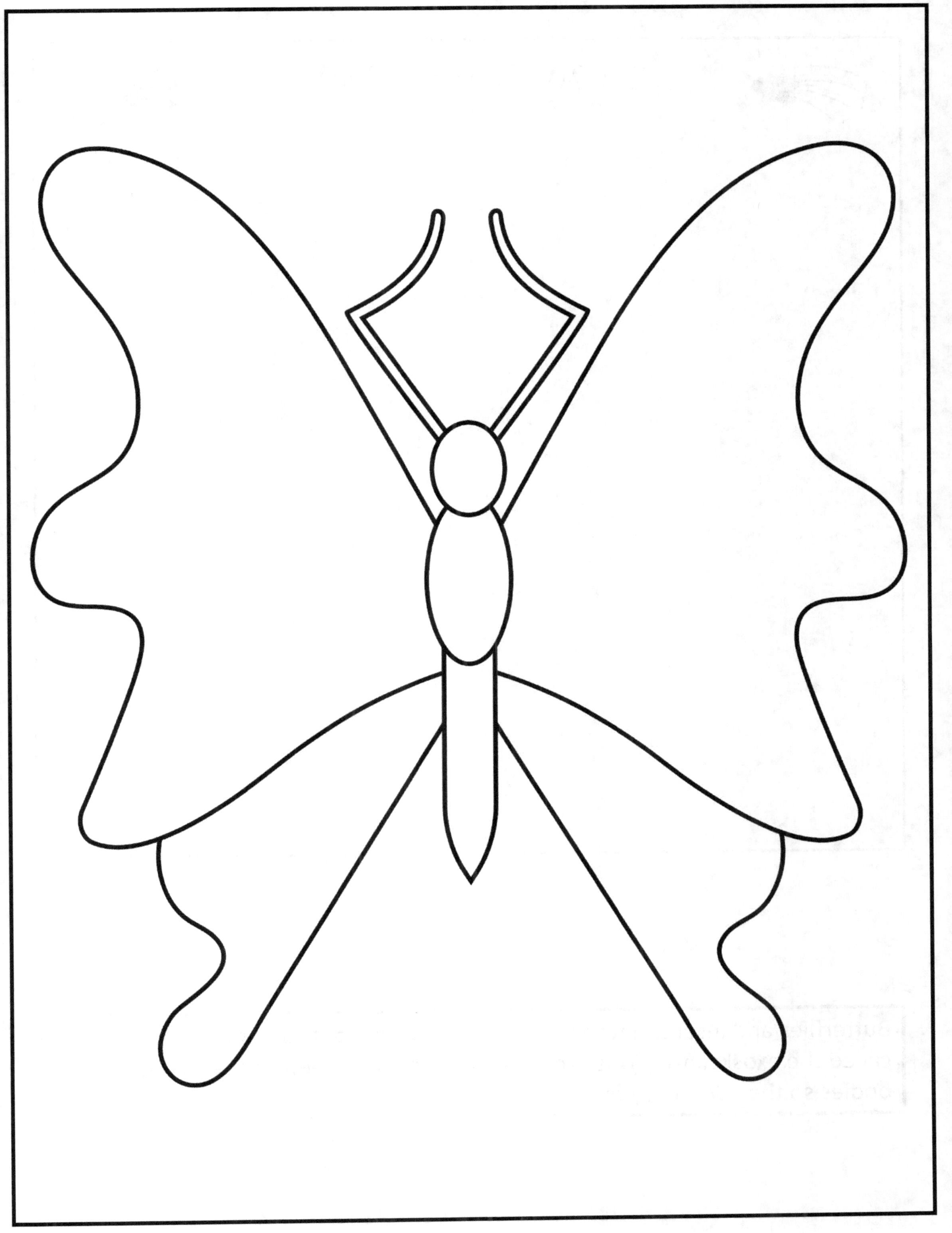

Draw something

Butterflies and insects have their skeletons on the outside of their bodies, called the exoskeleton. This protects the insect and keeps water inside their bodies so they don't dry out.

BUTTERFLIES
Coloring Book

Hello there

Thank you for choosing our book . We hope you love it! If you do, would you consider posting an online review? This helps us to continue providing great products and helps potential buyers to make confident decisions.

Thank you again for your support.